Benedict Arnold
A Drama of The American Revolution in Five Acts

by
Robert Zubrin

To Maggie

Benedict Arnold
A Drama of the American Revolution in Five Acts

Polaris Books
11111 W. 8th Ave., Unit A
Lakewood, CO 80215

www.polarisbooks.net

Copyright © 2005 Robert Zubrin
All rights reserved, including the right of reproduction in whole or in part in any form.

Manufactured in the United State of America
First Polaris Book Edition 2005
ISBN 0-9741443-1-2
LCCN 2004099937

Layout and Cover
Alien Perspective

Please contact us for pricing on orders of 10 or more copies.

Dramatis Personae

Major General Benedict Arnold
Major John Andre, British Adjutant General
Peggy Shippen (later Peggy Arnold)
General George Washington
Colonel Alexander Hamilton, aide to Washington
Marquis De Lafayette
Sir Henry Clinton, British Commander in Chief
Colonel John Jameson (U.S.)
Joseph Reed, President of Pennsylvania
Major Benjamin Talmadge (U.S.)
Colonel Richard Varick, aide to Arnold
La Luzerne, the French Ambassador
Elizabeth Schuyler, betrothed to Hamilton

American Partisans ("Skinners"):
John Paulding, Issac Van Wart, David Williams

US:
Soldiers, Officers, a Lieutenant, Three Sergeants, A Messenger, Three Councilors, Three Patriot Girls

French:
Two Officers

British:
Two Officers, Three Tory Girls, Servant Girl

ACT I

Act I   Scene I   **Saratoga Field 1777**

(*Enter Gen. Benedict Arnold*)

Arnold
Was ever a man so wronged as I,
I, Benedict Arnold?
Was ever a man so put upon?
Here I stand on Saratoga field,
Which should be my field of glory.
But I, a Major General yet stript of command
must meekly watch,
While Burgoyne, whose once mighty host
My sword brought to his current catastrophe but yesterday,
Today grinds out his last hopes,
And with a few more twitches of his dying army,
Hands the laurels of immortal victory to General Gates,
Who now is in sole command.

Gates, useless General Gates.
No soldier, but a conspirator,
Who, while the cause was in its darkest hour,
Plotted his ambition against Washington.

Washington! There's a great soul, a wise mind.
He knows the truth.
I have his letters here.
While a world of liliputians, civilians, speculators, and complainers,
Berate me for my failure before Quebec,

(cont.)

Arnold (cont.)
He honors me.
For he knows men and war.
And sometimes I even think
That placed in the admiration of that one wise mind,
My honour might rest secure,
Despite the rest.
But oh, to have succeeded before Quebec!
Then I, like Cortez with a band minute,
Had seized an empire;
To the marvel of all future ages.
And should they not marvel still,
That I, with a band so small,
Did storm the plains of Abraham?
And might have stormed the plains of heaven,
Did not the merest chance of a pitched night's desperate battle
Deny the golden prize.
And now I must watch,
While my twice earned glory is stolen again.
This time not by British bullets fired in the night,
But in the daytime intrigues of a clever fellow officer,
Who, discharging me, plans to receive Burgoyne's
surrender and take sole credit for a victory
He could never have won.

(*Alarms, retreat*)

But what is this?

(*Enter panicked American soldiers*)

Soldier
Hessians! Run for your life!
(*exit, other side*)

Arnold
What? A rout?
Is this Gates so weak
That he cannot hold the ripe fruit of victory
when placed in his very hand?
Is the triumph of a campaign to be turned to dust in a single afternoon?
I will not have my work so confounded.

(*Enter American Lieutenant with several soldiers, retreating.*)

1st Soldier
It's General Arnold.

Arnold
(*to Lt.*)
Sir, what is the meaning of this retreat?
Who ordered it?

Lieutenant
Sir, no one has any orders.

Arnold
(*aside*)
No orders!

Lieutenant
But the British have launched a mighty attack.
Our line is broke and must withdraw. The day is lost.

Arnold
Lost? Are you mad?
Lieutenant, men, you are running before shadows.

(cont.)

Arnold (cont.)
The British are at their ration's end,
This is but a death rattle.
But twill be your death rattle
If you let them out of this present trap.
Resupplied with victory, their savage allies will return.
And while you run and hide,
Throughout the valleys of the Hudson and the Mohawk,
Not even Tory girls will be safe from rape and pillage.
So hideous will be the result if you flee this day.
But why flee?
See how slow the British move to follow?
They have no powder,
Their strength is paper thin.
A single thrust will crumple them.

Are you men owed pay?
(*All nod*)

Well, behind that wall of paper men lies Burgoyne's camp,
And in it, gold enough to settle all accounts.
Behind which will flow all the gold in France.
For 'tis certain, that with Burgoyne's surrender will come
The aid of France, and with it
Victory, peace, and heavenly felicity.
So that's it boys, Heaven or Hell.
If you want salvation
You'll have to seize it at the point of sword or bayonet
and rip it from those British lines.

I'm ready to try, boys,
Are you with me? (*draws*)

2nd Soldier
I'd follow you against any British troop, General Arnold!

Arnold
There's a man! And the rest?

3rd Soldier
(*Fixing his bayonet*)
And I through their entire force,
Or hell itself, lead on!

Arnold
Brave boys! Very well Lieutenant, Sound the charge!

Lieutenant
Yes sir!
(*signals, a drumbeat and charge are sounded*)

Arnold
To Burgoyne's camp! Charge!

Soldiers and Lieutenant:
Huzzah!
(*All charge off*)

Benedict Arnold is wounded leading the final charge to victory at Saratoga. Engraving of original painting by Chappel.

Act I   Scene II

(*Scene: Washington's camp near Philadelphia. Music, Yankee Doodle, sounds of fireworks, celebration. Enter Washington, Lafayette, and Colonel Alexander Hamilton*)

Washington
What news Gentlemen! What glorious news!
Burgoyne is taken. Thousands of prisoners! And all confirmed!

Hamilton
It might have been confirmed several days earlier had Gates shown you the courtesy of dispatching the news to you direct, instead of reporting only to Congress.
What an insult.

Washington
Colonel Hamilton, in exchange for such news, I'll gladly grant Gates his little affronts. But have no fear, when the truth is known, Gates will be able to make no more capital out of this than he justly merits.

Lafayette
Gates' report did not mention the heroism of General Arnold.

Hamilton
But Schuyler's did, as will a thousand others.
The truth in this will not be hid.

Lafayette
And when it's out, Gates' bragging will be seen most ungraceful.

Washington
Yes. But to more important things. How is Arnold?

Hamilton
Badly wounded in the assault. He may lose a leg. But the surgeon says he is strong and should live.

Washington
Pray for his speedy recovery, Gentlemen, for we dearly need men of his calibre. If he lives, I'll see he gets the most important posts his recuperation will allow.
What a man, What a soldier, What a patriot!

Act I Scene III

(*Scene: a drawing room in Philadelphia. Enter Captain John André, Peggy Shippen and servant girl. He is drawing her. She sings "The Banks of the Dee." The servant girl accompanies her on the piano.*)

Peggy
(*singing*)
'Twas summer and softly the breezes were blowing,
And sweetly the nightingale sang from the tree.
At the foot of the hill where the river was flowing,
I sat myself down by the banks of the Dee.
Flow on, lovely Dee, flow on thou sweet river,
Thy banks, purest stream, shall be dear to me ever,
For there I first gained the affection and favor,
Of Jamie, the glory and pride of the Dee.

But now he's gone from me and left me this morning,
To quell the proud Rebels, for valiant is he.
But ah! there's no hope of his speedy returning,
To wander again on the banks of the Dee.
He's gone, hapless youth, o'er the rude roaring billows,
The kindest, the sweetest of all his brave fellows,
And left me to stray 'mongst these once-loved willows,
The loneliest lass on the banks of the Dee.

But time and my prayers may perhaps yet restore him,
Blest peace may restore my dear lover to me;
And when he returns with such care I'll watch o'er him,
He never shall leave the sweet banks of the Dee.

(cont.)

Peggy (song cont.)
The Dee then will flow, all it's beauty displaying,
The lambs on its banks will again be seen playing,
Whilst I, with my Jamie, am carelessly straying,
And tasting again all the sweets of the Dee.

(*The song ending, she beckons for the servant girl to leave, who does so.*)

Peggy Shippen 1777, Drawing by John André

André
My dear Peggy, yours are the features of a natural
aristocrat. Such a divine little mouth, sweet even to gaze upon,
such a finely chiseled nose, upturned from all things common.
When this dreary war is over, you must come with me, to shine in
all the courts of Europe.

Peggy
Promised like a soldier.
(*smiling*)
But tell me, Captain André, why to Europe, where in courts I
would be but common, while here I am admired almost like a
Queen?

André
You underrate yourself, dear Peggy. In Europe you would be
worshipped. Princes, Dukes, and Counts would fall at your feet,
begging to do your bidding. It would be a crime for a gem like
you to remain in America among these filthy mobs. The stench of
Americans must turn every aristocrat's stomach, such that I think I
myself would have died, had not a sweet haven been provided for
me in this, your perfumed, delicious arbor.
There is no way such a finely cultured goddess as yourself could
endure life among such canaille.

Peggy
(*turning and pulling out a pocket dictionary*)
(*aside*)
Canaille?...Oh!
(*smiles and admires herself in a mirror...There is a thud and flash
of fireworks at the window.*)
Oh John, look, a rocket! Are the canaille attacking?

André
(*continuing to draw*)
No my dear, I'm afraid the rocket signifies far worse.

Peggy
Worse?

André
Yes, I'm afraid the rebels are celebrating.

Peggy
Then the rumors are true?

André
Yes, (continuing to draw) Burgoyne has surrendered.

Peggy
To the canaille? Men of quality beaten by common canaille?

André
Yes. 'Tis but the chances of war.

Peggy
But what does it signify? Surely the war is not lost? Your army forced to leave Philadelphia? The great ball cancelled?

André
Tut. This war cannot be lost. And if, as it seems, that come spring our army must briefly leave this fair city, the ball will not be cancelled, but expanded. To remind the fairest of Philadelphians of our lovely stay and present return.

Peggy
Then you will be leaving.

André
Yes...too soon. And dear Peggy, it distresses me greatly to think of the trials you will be subject to here for our sake. Come with us to New York.

Peggy
And live the life of a refugee?

André
A gay one.

Peggy
No, I'll stay here, endure what comes, and treasure your memory till you come back.

André
(thinking) There are many fine gowns in New York.

Peggy
From Paris?

André
From London and Paris both. Gowns such as great ladies wear.

Peggy
(*first looking at herself in the mirror and then coming close to André*)
If you could send me one...

André
Say no more, I'll send three.

Peggy
Oh John, I love you. If only I could do something to show I was worthy of you so you <u>would</u> take me back to Europe with you.

André
You are more than worthy. But if you want to do something to help me, you may soon have a chance.

Peggy
How? Just name the way, and if a woman may do it with honour, it will be done.

André
It may be dangerous. I fear to expose such a frail creature to danger.

Peggy
If it can help you, I fear no perils.

André
Well then; you know I am the Army's chief officer for the procurement of information.

Peggy
Yes.

André
When the enemy army is here there will be many gallant officers, and much that a beautiful woman of strong
character can discover.

Peggy
Yes! Fear not, Captain André. The canaille officers will be like putty in Peggy Shippen's hands. I'll make them brag their all, and whatever they say I'll write to you in secret ink, on the same sheets I send you to order more gowns.
But it grows late. I must retire. I'll look forward to accompanying you at the ball.
Good night, sweet Captain.

(*Peggy exits*)

André
Good night, sweet...spy. And the sweetest of spies are surely the best.

Thus all my traps are laid
Which shall bring the dung born rebels to their pitiable end.
Wealth rules, not reason.
See this pretty little bird?
Her cousin is chief of doctors to Washington's force.
A scholar, a man of science,
Of courage, distinction and repute,
A healer.
Nay, what though he had assisted her very birth!
We shall hang him like a dog.
And she shall help us.
What more need I do than stroke her feathers,
And she obeys without a thought.
She shall be my glove,
A beautiful glove to mask my iron hand.
With such a glove as lure,
What fine fond hero might not place himself in my grasp?
Time will tell, and this is but a sample
Of what I have sown.
I shall win this war.
The fleets and Hessians are just for show.
Thus it has always been;
Since time immemorial, the herds of rats of common men
Had always far more force than needed to whelm over the well bred.
But they don't. For beasts are but beasts.
And a little bait here, and a little bait there,
And their poor little minds are quite confounded.

(cont.)

André (cont.)
And ours to determine.
Burgoyne was a fool to try his strength with brutes.
That brutes can fight, oh 'tis most certain;
As certain it is that think they cannot.
To their stomachs and groins they are slaves,
And their stomachs and groins are ours to command.
So must corrupt men always be ruled.
Of what use were all of Cromwell's victories once Monk was bought?
Thus shall it be with Washington.
Already numbers of his captains my receipt books do know,
For gold may flow where swords may never go.

(*exit*)

ACT II

Act II Scene I   1778

(*Scene: Philadelphia, the Ball in honour of the arrival of the French Ambassador. Enter from opposite sides 4 Patriot Girls including Elizabeth Schuyler, and 4 Tory Girls including Peggy Shippen. French and American officers, including Hamilton and Lafayette are in the background chatting and toasting. Ball music is playing. The Tory Girls have high coiffures, low cut dresses, and are much more elaborately dressed and bejewelled than the Patriot Girls, of whom Elizabeth is the best dressed. The Patriot Girls lack the high coiffures, wear nice modest dresses and red, white and blue ribbons in their hair. Peggy is clearly the richest of all.*)

Patriot Girl #1
Look at those Tory girls, they're shameless!

Patriot Girl #2
Hussies! Why were they invited anyway, Elizabeth?

Elizabeth
Policy, I hear. A grand ball is called for to welcome the French ambassador, so our very fashionable sisters, the Tory belles, had to be invited to add their glitter. But fear not. Men are not deceived by their vanities. Our officers will always prefer virtue to fashion.

(*They nod.
The music changes signifying the beginning of a dance.*)

Patriot Girl #3
Oh! It's the waltz.

(*Hamilton and Lafayette walk over to the Patriot Girls, Hamilton taking Elizabeth, Lafayette another Patriot Girl. All the other men, however, walk over and try to get a Tory Girl partner. There are not enough Tory Girls to go around. The leftover men reluctantly cross the floor to take Patriot Girl partners. The dance begins. The Patriot Girls look warmly on their partners, the Tory Girls look coldly into space. The officers dancing with the Tory Girls look ardently on their partners. The officers (except Hamilton and Lafayette) dancing with the Patriot Girls are constantly stealing glances at the Tory Girl Couples. They constantly split from their partners to butt in on officers dancing with a Tory Girl. The displaced officers then reluctantly take a Patriot Girl, etc. The Patriot Girls get more and more frustrated, one stepping on her partner's foot to gain his attention, etc. Finally the dance ends, and the parties divide as before.*)

Patriot Girl #3
You were saying something about virtue and fashion?

Elizabeth
They waver when dazzled, but will return to duty. These Tory girls are very chilly companions.

Patriot Girl #2
Well, I know one young officer whose due for a defrosting he'll never forget.

Officer
Ladies and Gentlemen, Major General Benedict Arnold, Commandant of Philadelphia!

(*Enter Arnold, on crutches. The men shake his hand, etc., and return to their business. The women, except Peggy and Elizabeth crowd around him and help him to a chair where they continue to vamp on him. The Patriot Girls listen intently, the Tory Girls giggling. Arnold pays increasing attention to the Tory Girls. Hamilton and Elizabeth cross the stage to confront Peggy Shippen.)*

Elizabeth
So Peggy dear, have you met my fiance, Colonel Alexander Hamilton?

Hamilton
Delighted to make your acquaintance, Miss Shippen.

Peggy
(*Lets him kiss her hand in so disdainful a way she practically slaps him in the face*)
Charmed. Well you certainly have done well for yourself, <u>Mister</u> Hamilton.

(*She is so cold that Hamilton shrinks away to talk with Arnold intermittently through the latter's group of admiring females.*)

Elizabeth
(*counter attacking*)
Isn't it wonderful! Now that we have secured the French alliance the war will soon be over, and the British forever driven from our shores.

Peggy
Yes, delightful. And to think of all the wonderful gifts this revolt has brought to so many. Take our commandant General Arnold for example.

(*The crowd listens in.*)

Who would have thought that a drugstore apprentice would rise to such eminence.

(*Arnold and the Patriot Girls are shocked, the Tory Girls giggle, Hamilton smiles at his friend's discomfort.*)

Peggy
And your charming fiance, Mister or Colonel, as you call him, Hamilton.
Who would ever have thought the son of one Rachel Levine and an unknown West Indies vagabond might marry a Schuyler?
Tell me, do you think the children will be black or white?

(*Hamilton reddens, Patriot Girls are shocked, Elizabeth walks off in a huff, Tory Girls giggle, and Arnold guffaws.*)

Arnold
That girl has spirit!
Miss Shippen!

Peggy
(*looks at him*)
Yes, General Arnold?

Arnold
(*pause...at a loss for words*)
Miss Shippen, I would like to make your acquaintance.

Peggy
So would I, were I you.

Arnold
Miss Shippen, you have a very haughty manner. Where did you learn it?

Peggy
Not in a drugstore.

Arnold
No, I can see that.

Peggy
Tell me, General, this wound of yours, I hope it won't interfere with your resuming your drugstore trade after the war?

Arnold
Well, actually I was not planning on engaging in drugstore trade after the war.

Peggy
No?

Arnold
No, I was thinking about living like a baron on one of the confiscated Tory estates in upper New York.

Peggy
A noble ambition, but only a dream, as it requires defeating the British.

Arnold
We shall defeat them.

Peggy
(*moving closer, displacing others, focusing Arnold's attention on herself*)
And you General, how soon will you again be ready to engage your person in combat with the forces of the King?

Arnold
I suppose it would depend on the type of combat. For certain varieties, I would be ready now.

Peggy
(*flirtatiously*)
You have suffered so much already. The King's forces can be very cruel to those who fall into their hands. Do you
really feel yourself brave enough for another encounter?

Arnold
To achieve my dreams I am prepared to brave any cruelty, Miss Shippen.

Peggy
Well, we shall see, General Arnold.

(*exeunt*)

Act II Scene II

(*Scene: Peggy's drawing room. Enter Peggy Shippen and a Tory Girl.*)

Tory Girl
What an oafish suitor this Arnold is. These letters he writes you are past laughter.
(*reads giggling*)
"Twenty times have I taken my pen to write you and as often has my trembling hand refused to obey the dictates of my heart. A heart which has often been calm and serene amid the clashing of arms, and all the din and horrors of war..."

Peggy
Modest, is he not?

Tory Girl (*continuing*)
"Trembles with diffidence and the fear of giving offence when it

(cont.)

Tory Girl (cont.)
attempts to address you on a subject so important to its happiness. "Long have I struggled to efface your heavenly image from it. Neither time, absence, misfortunes, nor your cruel indifference have been able to efface the deep impression your charms have made. And will you doom a heart so true, so faithful, to languish in despair?

Peggy
Yes!

Tory Girl
"Shall I expect no returns to the most sincere, ardent and disinterested passion?"

Peggy
The poor thing!

Tory Girl
"Dear Peggy, suffer that heavenly bosom, which surely cannot know itself the cause of misfortune without a sympathetic pang…"

Peggy
(*holding her heart*)
Pang! Oh Pang! Pang! Pang!

Tory Girl
"To expand with friendship at last, and let me know my fate."

Peggy
(*Thumbs down*)

Tory Girl
"If a happy one, no man will strive more to deserve it. If on the contrary, I am doomed to despair,…"

Peggy
And doomed you are!

Tory Girl
"My latest breath will be to implore the blessing of heaven on the idol and only wish of my soul."
(falling to her knees in mock worship)

Peggy
How sweet.
And best of all, the confused clod knows not that Betsey Deblois, his former idol, and I, are confederates, and can compare his desperate refrains of passionate love to her and me, and amuse ourselves with the tradesman's economy, seeing how he uses each letter twice, with but the names changed.

Tory Girl
And yet, the low-born clown does in truth swoon for thee.

Peggy
Yes I know. The poor fish is hooked. I have him on my string, and can now play him for amusement.

Tory Girl
Oh, play him to distraction. Jerk him about. Now you have him in your power, be an avenger for us all on these louts who have overtaken our country.
Oh, my carriage is here, I must depart.
(exit)

Peggy
Never fear. This drugstore fish shall be sorely tried, And after proper spicing, fried.

(exit)

Act II Scene III

(*Scene: Pennsylvania Supreme Council. Enter President Joseph Reed and 3 Councilors*)

Reed
I tell you, gentlemen of Pennsylvania's Supreme Council, it's a scandal. This General Arnold conducts himself after the fashion of a British aristocrat.

1st Councilor
President Reed is right. When Lord Howe commanded the city he kept not half so luxurious an establishment.

2nd Councilor
How can he afford it?

3rd Councilor
He's profiteering. The proof stands naked. He trades with New York Tories for scarce goods and uses government wagons for his own transport. All to get the wealth he needs to live as one among the Tory rich.

2nd Councilor
Yes, that is what I cannot understand, the way he nuzzles the Tories so, judging in their favor on every occasion, and in all affairs conducts himself to please them, and not us.

1st Councilor
He is the captive of the high born Shippen girl.

2nd Councilor
In love?

3rd Councilor
The chains she holds him by are made not of love, but of ambition.

Reed
Correct. His own infernal ambition.
An ambition such as Caesar's
Which would end our republic
As Caesar's ended Rome's.
Gentlemen of the Council,
We are the guardians of the people's freedom.
Our hatred of Arnold's arrogance
Is based not on envy,
But on duty.
Such Crimes must be cut off and condemned
If the Republic is to survive.
I ask for a bill of indictment.

2nd Councilor
But Arnold is a Hero. And while we here know of his crimes, it is only by word of mouth, and such weak proofs as would never carry a trial in battle with the General's reputation.

Reed
Then we shall spoil his reputation, while prolonging trial.
Day by day the ink of our newspapers shall blacken his name
Until his repute shall be buried in oblivion.
And convicted or no,
He shall flee this city
In dishonor and disgrace.

2nd Councilor
I suppose it is the prudent course.

Reed
It is the necessary course. Liberty itself is at stake.
Well Gentlemen, are we in agreement?
(*all nod*)
Then to our friends and allies let us go, and begin the ending of this aspiring tyrant.

(*exeunt*)

Joseph Reed, President of Pennsylvania and political nemesis of Arnold. Painting by Charles Wilson Peale.

Act II Scene IV

(Scene: Peggy's drawing room. Enter Peggy)

Peggy
How amusing this is.
The more desperately he seeks to enter into my affections,
The more all his former friends hate him;
Leaving him no choice but to kneel more abjectly to me,
Seeking our acceptance.
Thus poor General, you cut off your own retreat,
While I gently lead you to wrack and ruin.
And, poor fish, when finally pulled entirely out of the water that is your element,
You shall be thrown away on the beach
To writhe in agony as your life ebbs on the sand;
While circling high above you, joyously,
The plumed birds mock your dying torment.
How proud André would be,
If only he knew the wreckage
I have thus performed on the victor of Saratoga.
And wreck he now is;
Mine to sink at leisure or
Keep as prize?

Now there's a thought.
At Sea, Prizes are always kept.
They double the worth of the victory;
The enemy's loss is your gain.
What might I do
With a rebel Major General as my slave?
For surely I will soon have more power over him
Than ever woman held over man.

(cont.)

Peggy (cont.)
Might I not bring the rebel cause to total ruin
With their best General at my command?
Whatever their chiefs decide he knows,
Thus I would know, and so André would know,
And in securing the royal triumph, rise,
And be forever in my debt.

Of course, the thought repels
That I should be wed to a drugstore clerk.
But what of that;
When the war's won I'll have the marriage nulled;
And the princess shall kiss her pet frog goodbye,
To replace him with her charming Prince André.
Thus I am resolved.
But look who comes.

(*Enter servant girl*)

Servant Girl
General Arnold is here again to see you.
Shall I tell him to go?

Peggy
No, Show him in.

Servant Girl
Yes, Miss Shippen.

(*exit Servant. Enter Arnold, limping but without crutches*)

Arnold
I trust you are feeling well today Madam.

Peggy
(*smiling warmly*)
Oh, I feel <u>very</u> well. General, come here and sit by me.

Arnold
(*aside*)
Here's a strange change in the climate. I came here dressed for winter and now spring bids me unbutton.

(*He sits by her. She moves up close talking sweetly into his face.*)

Peggy
General, tell me about Saratoga.

Arnold
(*aside*)
This is wondrous strange.
(*to Peggy*)
But Miss Shippen, you always gave me to understand you were bored by military affairs.

Peggy
Call me Peggy. Not if they're yours. I want to know all about your battles. The way the rabble on the Council nip at your heels has made it clear to me that you are no ordinary man. You have done great things and are capable of doing more. That's why they hate you, and why I love you and want to know all about you, about your struggle to maintain order here in Philadelphia against this mob council, about your victories at Valcour Island and Saratoga. Tell me everything. (*fondling his neck*)

Arnold
(*aside*)
I will, but to my reason, <u>this</u> battle reminds me more of Quebec.

An easy entrance is found into a mighty fortress.
Is the fort taken, or have you walked into a trap?
It's night, there is no light;
Your eyes are of no use.
This girl who sits so warmly before me now,
Has stood these many months before as a cold proud tower,
And her I have sieged with as much abandon as I sieged Quebec.
Now she opens. But once inside, do you find a prize to be grasped;
Or do the walls of the impregnable citadel become
Your unbreakable prison,
Where, with no escape,
Your hopes are drowned in the hell of your comrades' blood.
Yet there is no point sieging unless you will cross the walls;
And let chance decide if it is here that Arnold falls.

(*Turns to talk softly to her. Exeunt arm in arm*)

ACT III

Act III   Scene I
(*Scene: Arnold's mansion in Philadelphia*)

(*Enter Arnold*)
Arnold
This woman is a strong persuader
And has swept me out with her tide.
But tho' quit of my whiggish moorings
I am not minded yet
To anchor my craft on the other side,
And so am I now adrift.
To be seen as traitor by the brave boys I have led,
That were shame I would avoid.
But to stay among these men,
Where daily my name is dragged through the mud,
And piled with dishonour
By clever men,
Who turn my every reply to their vantage,
Till defenseless I am scorned and pointed at in the streets.
This I cannot endure.
I am innocent of these charges.
Well, almost innocent.
That I have profiteered 'tis true,
But others have done the same.
Nay — some of my accusers have done more.
Should merchants be enriched while wounded soldiers are made poor?
They want for free what I have fought to win.
And at bottom, they lack proof.
Which is why, subtle lawyers that they are, they stall trial.

(cont.)

Arnold (cont.)
Fair trial I must have, and soon,
To clear myself, regain my repute,
And take the field again for America, with honour.
But if such is to be, it must be quick;
For this Tory witch with her powers and spells
Pulls me hard the other way,
Where soon I will be fastened.
Already we have sent a messenger to this André she knows,
Clinton's aide,
To discuss my serving the crown.
And he says, I should come not over as an honorable
soldier in my own person
But rather, while in service to Congress,
I should foully betray a division of men into Clinton's hands,
Then to be "rewarded beyond my expectations."
Perhaps for such infamous service the British shall reward me
beyond my expectations in the same way the patriots have already
rewarded my more noble deeds.
Then would Arnold indeed be a pitiful wreck.
Thus I'll write Washington.
(*writes*)
"For heaven's sake, let me be immediately tried and if guilty
executed. I want no favor; I only ask justice. Let me beg of you
sir, to consider that a set of artful, unprincipled men in office
may misrepresent the most innocent actions, and by raising a
public clamour against Your Excellency, place you in the same
disagreeable situation I am in.
Having made every sacrifice of fortune and blood, and
become a cripple in the service of my country, I little
expected to meet the ungrateful returns I have received
from my countrymen. I have nothing left but the little
reputation I have gained in the Army. Delay in the present case is
worse than death."
(*sealing it*)

Arnold
There.
And here comes my hangman.

(*Enter Peggy*)

Peggy
(*aside*)
There he stands
My difficult husband.
For nigh a year
I have charmed him, reasoned him,
Nagged him and dragged him,
But still he does not move.
I have tied my life to this clod
To the sorrow of my parents and my own best hopes.
A useful burden he is,
For I have made of him a shield
For the Shippen family, friends, and all our loyal kind
From the fury of mobs and demagogues.
But tis not enough.
The fine world is dying,
The mansion is aflame,
And will burn to destruction
Unless the fire is soon put out.
This Arnold is coarse, but bold,
A man to deal the heavy sudden blows the times require.
Many hearts might follow his.
He has a rough but winning way.
(*her mood wavers*)
I've married him, will bear his child,
Am sworn to his obedience.
He is a brave warrior,
And if the fair must love the brave,

(cont.)

Peggy (cont.)
I could almost bring myself to love him,
If he did but fight for the right.
It is not my place to rule him,
Yet rule him I must, or count my life a waste.
For I mean to be a maker of my time,
And not its mere decoration.
Therefore, harden your heart to wifely love,
Peggy Shippen,
Your husband is the enemy to all you hold most dear
Till he be won over.
Besides, you were meant for better.
(*to Arnold*)
My dear General, I would have a word with you.

Arnold
(*aside*)
I know what she wants.
I cannot resist her with principles, so I will stall her with practicalities.

Peggy
Why do you wait so long in accepting André's offer?

Arnold
His terms are vague. I like them not.

Peggy
Vague? How?
He says your services will be warmly welcomed and amply rewarded. What's more to say?

Arnold
He names no price.

Peggy
What!
You mean to dicker over price with André, you store clerk!
Oh, I knew I shouldn't have married beneath myself;
Oh, the ladies were right about you!
To think I thought you a gentleman.
You're still just a clerk.

Arnold
Still, I would have a price.

Peggy
Clerk!

Arnold
Would you be poor?

Peggy
Certainly not, but we are rich.
The Shippen lands are vast, and I heiress to a third.

Arnold
And all to be seized by Congress once our treason is known.

Peggy
What matter that?
When the rebellion's crushed, the crown will return all.

Arnold
And should it not be crushed?
Would you live out your days on a refugee's pension?

Peggy
It will be crushed.

Arnold
It <u>might</u> be crushed.

Peggy
How say you "might?"
The King has more ships, more men, and more money.
His victory is certain. He cannot lose.

Arnold
Ships may be scattered by storms, men scattered by night,
And money scattered by men.
In war nothing is certain.
Anyone can lose.
<u>Chance</u> decides all.

Peggy
At Quebec and Saratoga you trusted yourself to Chance?

Arnold
Yes.

Peggy
So chance yourself now with André.

Arnold
No.

Peggy
Why not?

Arnold
There'll be chance enough in the doing of this affair.
I'll take no chance on the worth of the prize.

Peggy
(*aside*)
This storeclerk's reckoning is not entirely without sense.
And for my part, I know I can expect no courtship from André
unless I be well heeled.
(*to Arnold*)
What price would you ask?

Arnold
Five Thousand Pounds sterling, win or lose,
and a golden guinea for each soldier I hand over.

Peggy
...Five Thousand....That's too low.
Ask for ten thousand, and two guineas a man.
And we must be compensated for whatever lands and
properties I forfeit.

Arnold
Fine. So I'll write him thus
(*writing*)
and demand a general's commission in the King's army to boot.

Peggy
Is that necessary?...Oh, very well.
But having made ourselves so fair a claim, think you not that we
should make some gift, to show we bargain in earnest?

Arnold
You mean send some useful intelligence
as a token of our willingness to serve the crown?

Peggy
Yes, that is what I meant, in a merchant's metaphor.

Arnold
You seemed to have picked up the lingo quite nicely.
In any case, I will here add for André's perusal a few such secrets of our command as will quickly whet Clinton's appetite for our services.

Peggy
(*kissing him quickly*)
Good! Well I must get dressed.
Peggy Chew and I are going to the Theatre.

Arnold
Oh, what's showing?

Peggy
Anthony and Cleopatra.
(*exit*)

Arnold
And so it has always gone.
Well I'll write here some secrets of interest perhaps but no real value. Perchance in plumbing me for more, André's reply will give me view of the British plans.
If Washington succors me, that will stand me in good stead.
If not, why, ten thousand pounds and a royal rank,
Will keep me quite well fed.

(*exit*)

HMS Jersey in New York harbor. Over 5,000 American priosoners died in her hull.

Act III   Scene II

(*Aboard Prison Ship Jersey in British occupied New York City. Enter André with General Sir Henry Clinton. At the opposite end of the stage, two British officers are chatting quietly.*)

1st Officer
That perfidious sycophant André clings to Sir Henry
Clinton like a leech, sucking promotions.
Hardly has it been four years since he bought his first commission, yet he now has risen to Major and command of the King's intelligence for all of America.
Military renown has he none, except his foul massacre of captives at Paoli and Tappan which have brought nought but dishonour on our arms.
In thinnest exteriors only could he be thought a gentleman. To think that Sir Henry could be so swayed by this dandy with his Swiss bank.

2nd Officer
He sways him not as a banker.

1st Officer
No? Then how?

2nd Officer
As a lady.

1st Officer
As a lady?

2nd Officer
Yes. As a mistress does he wrap himself around, binding the Commander in chains of fleshy love. And many a night do they abide together exchanging sweetness in unnatural embrace.

1st Officer
I should have known, 'tis a flaw common among the high born. That aristocracy should be so shaped is most strange. Perhaps it is the price they pay Providence for greatness.

2nd Officer
Providence? Nay. It is but a character that has bred among them like bleeding sickness or rotten chins.

Clinton
So, my dear Major André, you see our problem here. A thousand rebels have we packed in this hold, and the cost of their upkeep is beyond counting. And at present rate, the press of new prisoners will force on us several more such establishments, and leave our treasury bare.

André
Why not just hang the peasants? I see no need to take so many prisoners.

Clinton
Ah yes. At Tappan you took none. Tell me of that.

André
With pleasure. At night we came, soundless, with sword and bayonet only, and took them by surprise. And, when roused from their sleep we had them all at the point, the cravens begged for mercy, proving to the satisfaction of all the counterfeit nature of Yankee courage, before we plunged in the blades to dispose of the dogs.

Clinton
Many of our officers did not approve.

André
They fear for themselves should they fall into rebel hands, but their fear and softness may cost us the war. Fire and sword should we use, and burn out this rebellion as one burns out a plague ship. And where we cannot spread fire, we must spread terror, to conquer the minds of the rabble left unkilled. Thus in battle the bayonet should be our only weapon, for a man killed with musket ball is but subtracted from the enemy list and easily replaced. But kill a man with cold steel, let him watch in that horribly long instant as the blade comes down to pierce his breast, then in that last moment will a shrill thought of helpless terror escape his mind and fly for leagues to enfeeble the brains of his fellows. I tell you, force is useless unless it also terrorizes.

Clinton
You're right of course, but since we are surrounded with officers of a conventional cast, the problem still besets us of an overflow of prisoners, which there must surely be a way to cheapen within the rules of war.

André
Well, one way known to science would be to grind bits of glass into the prisoners' flour, which upon eating, rips their entrails somewhat, and shortens the prison stay of the less fit among them.

Clinton
And does their expiration seem natural?

André
Oh yes, quite so. For if done moderately the coughing up of blood commences only gradually, so that the patient appears to weaken and die across a week or two just as in nature.

Clinton
And how many prisoners do you think we could handle in this way?

André
With a ship of this size, eight, maybe ten thousand a year could be so processed.

Clinton
Then that's our answer! I tell you André, I don't know what I'd do without you. Your wit is as dear to me as your other parts.
(*giving his hip a fondle.*)
But I heard you had some news for me.

André
Yes. As you're aware, I've had correspondence with the rebel general, Benedict Arnold. Well, he has finally named a price. For ten thousand pounds, compensation, and two guineas a man, he's willing to take a command and surrender it to us.

Clinton
Ten thousand?

André
Yes. I'm sure you'll agree that such a sum would be a mere pittance to pay for such a coup.

Clinton
This Arnold, isn't he the drugstore clerk?

André
Yes, the one who took Burgoyne. We can now take him.

Clinton
That would be splendid. But are you sure he is in earnest?

André
Oh yes, I have an agent who knows his every thought.

Clinton
Indeed, André, you are ingenious. But he has no command.

André
Yet he can get one, almost at his preference, upon application to Washington.

Clinton
At his preference you say? Well then write him and tell him that if he can gain command of the fort at West Point, and surrender that to us, I'll meet his price. With that fort, we'll command all the Hudson, and split the northern rebels from the south, then to defeat either at our leisure. Let this Arnold flatter himself, that he may be the Monk of this rebellion, to be rewarded as Monk was for restoring Royal rule over Cromwell's upstarts.

André
Your strategy in this affair will no doubt take you considerably farther, Lord Clinton.

Clinton
Yes, I do think so. And now, having settled the business of the day what say you we retire for a game of handball and then to more tender amusements?

André
With pleasure, my Lord.
(*exeunt*)

Sir Henry Clinton, Commander in Chief of British forces in North America

ACT IV

Act IV   Scene I   **Philadelphia 1780**

(*Enter, from opposite sides, Peggy and Arnold*)

Peggy
(*aside*)
This fond husband of mine has escaped his court martial with but a reprimand, but he shall not so easily escape me. I live in the highest style and have quickly spent all his little wealth, so that he is now but a ward of my family. Not merely to pay debts to others, but to pretend to manhood before me does he now desperately need gold, and with this as my whip I shall swiftly drive him into André's hands.

Arnold
They had the gall to reprimand me, my own brother officers! What an insult, that they, with whom I have shared years of peril, and led to victory through rivers of ice and rivers of blood, should now have chosen to credit these conniving civilians over me. But no matter, I am through with the lot of them now; I care neither for them nor their cause. My main concern now is money; I must have cash.
The British offer is fair, but to have men think me a traitor is a shame I would still avoid. There are other ways to wealth; one can cruise the seas for gold in a privateer, and claim a share of patriot's glory while reaping the riches of a string of British prizes.
I have sought such a post, but none has opened.
Still, I have a way out. There are other monarchs with as much money to spend as George III, yet have not such an odium attached to their service. Thus I go now to sell myself to Louis XVI of France, America's staunchest ally.

(*Enter, on Arnold's side, La Luzerne, the French Minister. He is bejewelled, powdered, perfumed and extremely elaborately dressed.*)

Luzerne
Ah, Jeneral Arnold, I have been expecting you.

(*He holds out his hand to be kissed. After hesitating a moment Arnold takes it and tries to kiss it, but sniffing the perfumes sneezes all over Luzerne instead.*)

Luzerne
(*recovering*)
Well, what can I do for the Jeneral?

Arnold
Your excellency, I wish to offer my services to the King of France.

Luzerne
But you are an Americain Jeneral. I do not understand, Monsieur.

(*His leaning towards Arnold almost causes Arnold to sneeze again, which Arnold restrains.
This sort of byplay continues throughout the interview.*)

Arnold
Your excellency, regrettably, the means required by my establishment cannot be supported in the Continental service, and so I wish to serve the King of France.

Luzerne
Strange. I would have thought that a man of your condition could be amply maintained on a Jeneral's salary.

Arnold
I am deeply in debt.

Luzerne
I see. Well, how much do you require, Monsieur?

Arnold
I would need ten thousand pounds immediately and a salary of a thousand a year, in return for which I would serve the King in any way required. Does the King wish to regain Canada for France? Then entrust me the command of a French Army and I'll not only take it for him, but afterwards, use my considerable influence among the American command to see they acquiesce.

Luzerne
(*amused*)
Jeneral, I understand your predicament, and I deeply sympathize with the plight of a former hero who now finds himself poor, but surely you must realize that debts cannot be paid off with the sale of wild dreams. You should have been more frugal. Public servants must live modestly. So take it as a lesson. Avoid display, always remembering that the simple, modest, virtuous life is the best. Well, I must leave you now. We are having a ball here tonight, and I must change into my formal clothes. Adieu, Jeneral. If there is anything else I can do for you, please feel free to call on me again. (*exit*)

(*Arnold shambles over to Peggy*)

Peggy
You needn't tell me what the French answer was; I told you they would refuse, didn't I?

Arnold
Yes, you did.

Peggy
Well, I suppose I have enough money to meet our expenses, but you'll have to give up that new carriage of yours; my father can lend me one of his, which you can use when out visiting. Too bad you're still afraid to take the British offer. To think that the man of vision I married should have become such a cripple.

Arnold
A man of vision would take the British offer? Would sell out?

Peggy:
Oh really now, sell out? Sell out what? Chaos? Of course the rabble will say what they will, but does a general look for approval from his underlings? Look at this country; it was happy once, under the King's rule. Now havoc reigns.
Demagogues with mobs hound peaceful citizens out of their homes; violence, bloodshed, famine! It will go on and on and on, unless some great man puts an end to it. You can be this country's savior. One swift blow from you could end this pandemonium. Where you lead, others would follow.

Arnold
(*pausing*)
That would be grand...But still, we must look to ourselves. Treason is a mighty risk, even for ten thousand pounds.

Peggy
Would you chance it for thirty thousand?

Arnold
Thirty thousand? Hah! I'd bet the devil my head for thirty thousand.

Peggy
So thirty thousand would decide you?

Arnold
Of course. For that kind of money I'd chance anything, and never look back. But that sum will never be offered.

Peggy
It has been offered.

Arnold
What? How?

Peggy
I have negotiated it. The offer is, thirty thousand, for West Point, and ten thousand even if we fail.

Arnold
Thirty thousand...pounds...To live in endless wealth applauded as the savior of the country...Oh...We will not fail.

(*exeunt*)

Act IV   Scene II

Scene: Washington's camp near Stony Point on the Hudson
(*Enter Washington, Lafayette, Hamilton*)

Washington
We'll position our force here, by the Hudson. From this strong place we can swing south to Jersey or east to Connecticut, depending on Clinton's move, and if the French arrive in time on Long Island, we can drop down the river to seize New York and take Clinton from behind should he face out to meet them.

Lafayette
A good plan, my General, but I fear my countrymen may be too slow for this army to endure the wait.

Hamilton
Too true. Sir, there's talk of mutiny about throughout the whole army. We lack any force to quell it.

Washington
I know.

Hamilton
Look, here comes the soldiers' committee; they're the ringleaders. We can arrest them, at least.

Washington
No, they must be spoken with.

(*Enter soldiers' committee, composed of three sergeants*)

1st Sergeant
General Washington...

Washington
Yes, soldier?

1st Sergeant
...General sir, we three represent the soldiers' committee of the Massachusetts, Jersey and Pennsylvania line, and are chosen to speak for the rest.

Washington
And what is it that you have to say?

1st Sergeant
Well, Sir, it's this. The men have not been paid a cent in real money in over a year. The merchants won't take Continental paper, so we're all in debt.

2nd Sergeant
We're not even getting our rations. There are warehouses of supplies in Pennsylvania, but they are all being shipped somewhere else.

3rd Sergeant
So while we starve here in rags, our farms back home are being foreclosed, and our wives and children left to beg from speculators who have made themselves rich by not lifting a hand to defend the country.

1st Sergeant
The men are resolved that the Army should march on Philadelphia and demand justice from Congress at musket point.

Washington
What you speak of is too true. I have known it, and it has grieved me beyond endurance. But you must not take this rash act you speak of.

1st Sergeant
We have no choice.

Washington
Yes, you do. You must put your faith in reason, and not in force. I have friends in Congress, and I have been writing them for some time on this matter. There are many patriots in Congress, some even former soldiers like yourselves. We are all committed to justice for this Army. Congress has no money now. It will someday, perhaps soon, even before victory if the Confederation is ratified. And I pledge you on my word of honour that I will not rest until the foreclosures are stopped, the Army paid in full, and all these wrongs righted.

1st Sergeant
You're asking us to put our fate in the hands of politicians, when it is now in our power to make them do us justice.

Washington
Men, I know you are not mutineers. I know all three of you. You were all at Valley Forge, were you not?

(*they nod*)

I saw you fight at Brandywine, and you at Princeton, and you (*pointing to the 1st Sergeant*)
Sergeant...Cooper, I believe, you were with me as long ago as Dorchester Heights. You are veterans of an army that future ages will wonder at, that you could have endured so much for Victory in a sacred cause. I tell you men, what Common Sense says is true, the sun has never shone on a more noble cause. We do have the power to begin the world anew. Men, I have a vision of what this nation may become should it achieve freedom. I know you have it too or you wouldn't have stood by me this long. Think of it, a

(cont.)

Washington (cont.)
nation where every man has an equal right to build a life for himself and his family; a government which exists not to enrich an aristocracy, but to ensure the happiness of all the people, because the people will run it; a land where men will kneel only to God, and where the truth can be spoken freely. A land free of tyranny, where none can be jailed without cause, the first in the history of the world. If you bring this to be, your glory will be eternal. And this, through your suffering and your courage you have almost done, for while I cannot promise, I tell you from my heart that I believe victory not far off. But your glory will be tarnished and all we have fought for made worthless should you now subject Congress to force. Was it really worth enduring so much, have so many of our friends given their lives, merely to see the King replaced by a military dictatorship?

2nd Sergeant
At least they could ship us some more rations.

Washington
The bulk of the available rations are being shipped south at my order.

2nd Sergeant
<u>Your</u> order??

Washington
Yes. Things are going badly for us in the south. The troops we have there are but raw militia. They cannot make do as you can; they need all the help they can get.
You see, gentlemen, I put great faith in you.

(*The Sergeants confer briefly.*)

1st Sergeant
General, we will convey all you have said to the committee. Lead where you will. There will be no mutiny.

(*Pause. Then Washington solemnly salutes them. They return the salute and exit.*)

Hamilton
Sir, you have performed a miracle.

Washington
Nay, I merely asked for one. It is they who have performed the miracle.

(*Enter Arnold, only very slightly lame*)

Washington
(*brightening*)
Now here's a sight for sore eyes.

Arnold
General Arnold reporting for duty, sir.

Washington
(*receiving him warmly*)
And your arrival could not be more welcome. General, I'm sure you're already acquainted with my aide, Colonel Alexander Hamilton, and the Marquis de Lafayette.

Lafayette
I am only slightly acquainted as yet with General Arnold's person, but well do I know of his military fame.

Washington
You shall soon be much better acquainted with both, Marquis. General Arnold, I have decided to appoint you to a post of honour.

Arnold
Thank you, sir.
(*aside*)
West Point!

Washington
General, you are to command the left wing of the Continental Army.

(*Arnold appears stunned*)

Hamilton
Command of the left wing! What an honour!

Lafayette
Indeed! General, that is a command I have dearly wished for myself, but allow me to be the first to congratulate you. I know that General Washington could not have chosen a better soldier.

Hamilton
Congratulations.

Washington
Congratulations, Arnold.

Arnold
But...but what of my request for West Point?

Washington
General Arnold, there is no need to think of that. I know it was

(cont.)

Washington (cont.)
only the cloud of this silly scandal that made you request such a modest post. I care not for that. Let this promotion make clear to all where I stand between an officer of your merit and a bunch of squabbling civilians.

Arnold
But think you that I am fit for such high command?

Washington
Most fit. Arnold, the war grows long and privation is making the men waver. We need to strike a blow that will restore their spirits. That's why I have chosen you.
Remember that night by the Delaware, when you and I planned the attack on the Hessian camp? Well do I remember it. All seemed lost. Our army a tiny defeated remnant, shivering in the December snow, waiting only for dismissal on the first of the year. The country on us had turned its back, every farmer seeking only for pardon from the British victors, who with high contempt had given up pursuit of us as a waste of time. Yet, you with your daring and I with my Hope saw in this the call for attack, and with the amazing boldness of one stroke did turn disaster's tide.
Hah! If only you could have been there for the event. What was it you had said..."catching drunken Dutchmen in their Christmas stockings?" Hah! 'Twas just as you predicted.

Arnold
(*aside*)
These warm memories appear to me now as reproaches.

(*to Washington*)
But now I am lame, and more fit for fortress duty than command in the field.

Washington
You're healthy enough. Why, before you're done, you'll be having me wishing all my generals were so lame.

Arnold
But in honesty, sir, I do believe myself more fit for command of West Point.

Washington
Forget this West Point, Arnold. 'Tis a post for a granny. You're a fighting general, sir. I have few such. Who else do I have that could get a force of militia to stand and outnumbered, fight to the death, as you did at Valcour Island? Who else but you has rallied a wavering force on the field to turn and strike a death blow at a British army, as you did to Burgoyne at Saratoga? Arnold, one more such blow will win us the war! And you're the man to do it! The French will soon land, so we'll have force enough, that, with them as anvil and you as hammer, we'll smash Clinton between and take New York!

Arnold
(*aside*)
And tenfold settle the score for Quebec. How I once prayed for such a chance for glory. Yet accept I cannot. My letters are in André's hands, and he can hang me by letting loose their news of my treason. That, Peggy, and the thirty thousand chain me to my present course. So I must now disgracefully dissemble.
(*to the others*)
But I tell you I am lame! I'm lame!
(*starts to limp pitifully all over the stage*)

Lafayette
Can it be that Arnold's wound has broken his spirit?

Hamilton
No, it is the torture of the scandal trial.

Washington
I know not what it is, but it is most sad to see. Perhaps though a spell in an easy command will restore him. General Arnold!

Arnold
(*finally pausing in his limping about*)
Yes sir?

Washington
Since your wound prevents you from assuming a command in the field, I grant your request and hereby appoint you to command of the fortress at West Point. Good luck.

Arnold
Thank your sir.

Washington
And now, let's to dinner. I want to tell you about my plans for the coming campaign.

Arnold
I'm sure I'll find them most interesting, sir.

(*exeunt*)

Act IV Scene III
(*Enter Arnold and Peggy*)

Peggy
So now you command at West Point. How wonderful!

Arnold
But there's a slight change of plan.

Peggy
How so?

Arnold
It appears that we will be visited at West Point at the end of September by an inspection party of high ranking American officers.

Peggy
And how does this alter our plans?

Arnold
Well, don't you think we should find out how much Clinton will be willing to pay for not only West Point and its garrisons, but the heads of Hamilton, Lafayette, and General George Washington?

Peggy
Oh darling, I'm so proud of you!
(*kissing him*)
Let's write André at once!

Arnold
Yes, let's.
(*Exeunt arm in arm*)

Act IV   Scene IV

(*Scene: A tavern in British occupied New York. Enter Sir Henry Clinton, André, and two British officers.*)

Clinton
Gentlemen, I have invited you here for a most special occasion. Tonight we will drink a cheerful farewell to our friend Major André,

1st Officer
(*to 2nd*)
Farewell to the parlour snake! I'll drink with good cheer to that!

Clinton
The Major will soon embark on a most daring adventure.

2nd Officer
(*to 1st*)
With whose daughter, I wonder?

Clinton
This very night, Major André will travel up the river and go behind rebel lines to bring us the plans to West Point and final victory in this blasted war!

(*The officers look to each other, slightly awed.*)

1st Officer
Alone behind enemy lines…Sir Henry, are you sure that André is the right man for this kind of thing?

Clinton
Quite sure.

2nd Officer
Major André, this is indeed a risky business. Are you not a little afraid?

André
Afraid? Hah!
(*aside*)
In truth I am, and more than a bit. But the risk is minute when matched against the prize, and a little bravado is called for now to win these bulletheads over to the ranks of my admirers.
(*To the others*)
Colonel Billings, you were with General Wolfe at Quebec in the last war. Were you at his table on the night before he gave his life in winning Canada for the Crown?

1st Officer
Indeed, I was.

André:
And what song did he sing?

1st Officer
A real soldier's song; "How stands the glass around."

André
Right! Well, I'll sing it for you now.

(*André stands up on the table and sings "How Stands the Glass Around." All wax enthusiastic.*)

André
(*singing*)
How stands the glass around?
For shame ye take no care, my boys,
How stands the glass around?
Let mirth and wine abound.
The trumpets sound,
The colors they are flying, boys,
To fight, kill, or wound,
May we still be found,
Content with our hard fate, my boys,
On the cold ground.

Why, soldiers, why,
Should we be melancholy, boys?
Why, soldiers, why?
Whose business is to die!
What, sighing? Fie!
Don't fear, drink on, be jolly, boys!
'Tis he, you or I!
Cold, hot, wet, or dry,
We're always bound to follow, boys,
And scorn to fly!

'Tis but in vain, -
I mean not to upbraid you, boys, -
'Tis but in vain,
For soldiers to complain:
Should next campaign
Send us to Him who made us, boys,
We're free from pain!
But if we remain,
A bottle and kind landlady
Cure all again.

2nd officer
There's a man!

1st Officer
Hurrah for André!

Clinton
Good luck, John!

André
(*tossing off his mug and exiting*)
Victory or Death!

(*The rest salute him with their glasses and then exit, other side.*)

André's journey to meet Arnold. Drawing by John André.

ACT V

Act V Scene I   Sept. 1780

(*Scene: Night in a small house above the bank of the Hudson. Enter Arnold and André.*)

Arnold
So, Major André, now the deal is struck; here are the fortress plans. Washington will be within Monday next; that very night you must strike. These approaches will I have left unguarded, granting your force a surprise entry. At first alarm, I will make sure of Washington and his aides with a small Tory guard I have brought within, and so, when then you launch a noisy diversion at this other point, there will I, without fear of overrule direct our mistaken defense.

André
And thus like ripened fruit will the fort and its defenders fall into our basket, with Washington and Lafayette reaped among the crop. How well they shall look hanging on the gibbet.

Arnold
Indeed.
(*aside*)
So it has come to this. I now will hang the only man I ever loved. I hate it, but do it I must, for treason has no bottom, but digs itself ever deeper. Treason for cash is petty; to stand proud I must amaze the world by singly securing the royal triumph, so Washington must die. Yet, strange to say, I care not. A numbness fills me; I feel myself a walking corpse, as if in killing Washington I have killed myself. But yesterday in coming here, my barge was attacked by a

(cont.)

Arnold (cont.)
British boat and deeply did I wish that some kind cannonball would grant me a hero's death, preventing this meeting. But now this hand is dealt; I will play it out, and whoever hangs, let them hang.

André
It grows light, I must return to my ship. Fear not, General, you may count on the King's forces
(*aside*)
to spigot you on a bayonet when we take your fort. For a night assault has many accidents, and I see no need to waste thirty thousand pounds on this low born pig. Besides, I have other employments for his wife.

(*Cannon fire is heard.*)

André
What's that?

(*Both rush to the windows*)

Arnold
It's Colonel Livingston's artillery battery firing on your ship.

André
The ship is hit!

Arnold
They're very good marksmen.

André
Look! She's hit again!

Arnold
By a howitzer shell, I think. Hmm, they've been trying for months to get that thing in working order.

André
Oh no! They're weighing anchor to escape downstream!

Arnold
I would have expected more of a fight from the British Navy.

André
They're gone! My god, I'm trapped here! How am I ever going to get back to New York?

Arnold
(*aside*)
Even tho' my fate in this risky venture be twined with his, it does amuse me to see this serpent squirm.
(*to André*)
Don't be afraid, Major, I'll have one of my most trusted men guide you by land to the British lines. Smith!

(*Enter Joshua Hett Smith. He has the air of a fool.*)

Smith
Yes, General?

Arnold
Smith, I have a mission for you of the utmost importance, a secret mission.

Smith
Oh goody, I love secret missions.

Arnold
Smith, this is John Anderson, who is in our intelligence service. You are to escort him without interference through our lines to New York.

Smith
A spy? Great! Just wait till everyone sees me escorting a spy on a secret mission. They'll never call me a Tory coward again.

André
Are you sure this man is competent?

Arnold
The best. The best.

Smith
Well, you should take off that British uniform. Many people around here aren't as perceptive as I am and might think that you are really a British officer.

André
(*to Arnold*)
But if I'm captured out of uniform, I could be tried as a spy.

Arnold
Fear nothing. Anticipating the present need, I have already written to Major Talmadge, who commands our forces of security below, that John Anderson is to be let through without hindrance. No man under our orders will stop you. This man is but your road guide.

André
(*relieved*)
Oh, I see. That's much better. Well then
(*changing jackets*)
till next Monday night, farewell!

Anold
Farewell.

(*Exeunt, Smith with André, Arnold the other way.*)

Act V Scene II

(*Scene: the Neutral Ground, wilderness between American and British lines. Enter John Paulding, Isaac Van Wart, David Williams. They are armed and very shabbily dressed; Van Wart wears the remains of a Hessian uniform, Paulding that of a refugee (Tory). They are Skinners, bandits vaguely in the American service.*)

Paulding
That Hessian garbs fits you well, Van Wart. Without it and that fancy lingo of yours, we would never have escaped from that British prison ship.

Van Wart
Ja, Diese Dutch sprech der Deutch sehr gutt.

Paulding
And now we'll avenge ourselves on them for our stay in that floating hell.

Williams
And in the best way too; here, in the neutral ground, under no law and no command, we'll take from the Tories as they have stolen from us, and enrich ourselves while fighting the war.

(*Enter André*)

André
What a magnificent day. The sky shines, the birds sing the sweetness of success. The rebel lines far behind, I now stride through the British end of the Neutral Ground, an area well patrolled by loyalists, and soon will be safe within our outposts.

Williams
He looks rich.

Paulding
Halt or we fire!

Van Wart
Schtop richt vere you are!

André
(*aside*)
A Hessian deserter, a refugee, these are Tory irregulars.
(*to them*)
Gentlemen, I hope you belong to our party.

Paulding
What party?

André
(*gesturing in the downstream direction*)
The lower party.

Paulding
Yes, we are.

André
I am glad to see you. I am an officer in the British service, and have now been on particular business in the country, and I hope

(cont.)

André (cont.)
you will not detain me. And for a token to let you know that I am a gentleman...
(*pulls out a big gold watch*)

Williams
A British officer, what a catch.

André
(*aside*)
They're rebels!
(*to them*)
Hah, Hah, I must do anything to get along. I mistook you for Tories. No, Gentlemen, I am an American special agent. Here is my pass from General Arnold.

Paulding
Damn Arnold's pass! You said you was a British officer. Where is your money?

André
Gentlemen, I have none about me.

Williams
You, a British officer, and no money! Let's search him!

(*They strip search him.*)

Williams
Hmm, fine clothes, a gold watch, but not much money. I reckon he's not an officer.

Van Wart
(*feeling under André's sock*) Und vat is dis?
(*pulling off the sock*) Papers.

(*He and Williams puzzle over them.*)

André
(*aside*)
Hah! The stupid peasants can't read.

Paulding
Let me see those. I can read. (*taking them*)
Weh ehst Po-int. West Point! This is a spy!

André
(*aside*)
You think I'm caught. Scum like these can always be bought.
Watch now the power of gold.
(*To them*)
Gentlemen, I'm sure we can reach an understanding.
Everyone fights wars for their own reasons.
Name a sum that you wish, and I'll arrange it paid to ransom my release.

Van Wart
Vun Hundred Guineas.

André
Done.

Williams
No, two hundred is what we want pay that, or hang.

André
Sir Henry Clinton will pay that.

Williams
Alright then, how can it be arranged so we know we'll get our money?

André
Simple. Two of you can hold me here while one goes to get the money.

Van Wart
Zounds gutt.

Paulding
I think this man is worth more than two hundred guineas.

André
Alright gentlemen, why quibble. Let's settle on an even thousand guineas. You'll all be rich men.

Williams
A thousand guineas! Let's take it!

Van Wart
Ja, Ja.

Paulding
No, by God, if you give us ten thousand guineas, you shall not stir a step!

Williams
No, John. Let's take the money.

Paulding
And give them the plans to West Point? After what we went through on their hell ship? Never!

Van Wart
(*thinking and backing about*)
Ja, John is richt. Dies prisoner schould be turnt in.

Williams
This is costly patriotism, but I'll go along. There may at least be a reward. But the next prisoner we take, we ransom; that's settled, right?

Paulding
Agreed. All right you, put on your clothes and let's march.

(*André picks up his clothes and all exeunt.*)

The capture of André, from 19th Century engraving.

Act V Scene III

(*Scene: an outpost of the Continental Army. Enter Col. John Jameson and Major Benjamin Talmadge.*)

Jameson
Major Talmadge, I'm glad to see you. For but yesterday an event so strange did happen at this post that it baffles my simple soldier's wit to understand. But perhaps you, a man who deals each day in secrets and codes, ciphers and spies, can this affair unravel.

Talmadge
I'll be pleased to give what service I can, Colonel Jameson.

Jameson
Well then, yesterday a spy was caught escaping our lines with plans for West Point, complete in every detail and latest change. How such plans were got, me thinks, is a mystery of grave consequence.

Talmadge
Indeed. But tell me, how was he caught?

Jameson
By three bandits, destitute men searching for loot, yet so good at bottom that when stripping him and finding plans in place of pounds, did refuse bribes of great sums of royal gold for his ransom.

Talmadge
Great sums you say? Then he must be a man of great importance, and his mission of the highest rank. What was his name?

Jameson
John Anderson.

Talmadge
John Anderson! Why for this very man I have here a letter from General Arnold commanding that he be let through our lines without hindrance.

Jameson
Then...

Talmadge
This can only mean that Arnold is in league with this spy and means to betray his command at West Point!

Jameson
Arnold a traitor!? It cannot be!

Talmadge
It must be! There is no other source for this letter or for these plans. Where is the spy now?

Jameson
God forgive me! Upon his capture, I naturally forwarded him by guard to General Arnold, preceded by a messenger to bear the news.

Talmadge
Disaster! Send some men to overtake this guarded spy. Anderson must be brought back here at once.

Jameson
Yes! I'll send my fastest officer and follow with a hundred of my best dragoons. This spy won't escape. But the messenger to Arnold cannot be overtook.

Talmadge
Then we must get word to Washington at once. Is he with the main Army at Tappan?

Jameson
Why no. The commander and his staff are traveling and by the morrow,… mean to visit at West Point!

Talmadge
Like lambs into the wolf's lair! Oh, treason most foul! All is clear now. Arnold means to kill them or make them captive when he betrays the fort, and doom all our hopes with a double blow.

Jameson
Then there's not a moment to be lost! Treason's dagger hangs over our General's head.

Talmadge
I'll go myself and ride like the wind!
On speed alone all must now depend.

(*Exit; galloping hooves*)

Jameson
Godspeed, Talmadge.

(*exit*)

Major Benjamin Talmadge, of the Continental Secret Service. Drawing by John Trumball.

Act V Scene IV

(Scene: Arnold's headquarters near West Point Enter Arnold and Peggy, Varick opposite; enter Hamilton, Lafayette, Elizabeth Schuyler, and two other ranking American officers.)

Arnold
Ah, Marquis De Lafayette, Colonel Hamilton, Miss Schuyler, Gentlemen, here so soon? What a pleasant surprise! Are you traveling with General Washington?

Hamilton
Yes, he should be here presently. We rode on ahead to help you prepare his reception.

Arnold
I thank you. I'm sure that with your help we can make tonight a most memorable occasion for the General.

Peggy
Indeed, you gentlemen can't imagine how happy your visit here makes us.
(*allowing them all to kiss her hand*)

Lafayette
I hope that Mrs. Arnold has not found life in this fortress boring?

Peggy
(*smiling flirtatiously at them all*)
Why no. Actually I have found many pleasing diversions here.

Hamilton
Does Mrs. Arnold intend that the reception here tonight should be a gay affair?

Peggy
Oh yes, very gay. Far more exciting, I think, than any of you might have thought possible.

Hamilton
Then would it please Mrs. Arnold if I invited my fiancé, Betsy Schuyler, to attend?

Peggy
Of course! Elizabeth, your presence here tonight would add greatly to my pleasure.

Arnold
A drink then! To the joy ahead! Colonel Hamilton, a song!

(*Hamilton and Elizabeth sing "Anacreon in Heaven." Arnold and Peggy join in singing the second verse. The final two lines are sung in the operatic style of "The Star Spangled Banner."*)

Hamilton (*singing*)
To Anacreon in heav'n, where he sat in full glee,
A few sons of harmony sent a petition
That he their inspirer and patron would be;
When this answer arrived from the jolly old Grecian –

Elizabeth (*singing*)
Voice, fiddle, and flute, no longer be mute,
I'll lend you my name and inspire you to boot;

Elizabeth & Hamilton (*singing*)
And besides I'll instruct you like me to entwine
The myrtle of Venus with Bacchus's vine.

Hamilton & Arnold (*singing*)
Ye sons of Anacreon, then join hand in hand:
Preserve unanimity, friendship, and love;
'Tis yours to support what's so happily planned:
You've the sanction of gods, and the fiat of Jove,

Peggy & Elizabeth (*singing*)
While thus we agree, our toast let it be,
May our club flourish happy, united, and free!

All Four (*singing*)
And long may the sons of Anacreon entwine
The myrtle of Venus with Bacchus's vine.

Elizabeth Schuyler, Portrait by Charles Wilson Peale.
Alexanfer Hamilton, engraving by H.B. Hail, Jr.

(*Enter Messenger*)

Messenger
Message for General Arnold.

Arnold
(*taking him aside and privately opening the letter with only a slight change of expression on his poker face*)
(*aside*)
Caught!
(*returns to poker face and casually folds letter and puts it in his pocket*)

Messenger
By the way General, I saw General Washington on the road less than a mile away. He should be here in just a few minutes.

Arnold
I thank you. There is refreshment for you around back.

(*Exit Messenger*)

Arnold
Excuse me, gentlemen, I must have a private word with my wife.
(*takes her aside*)
That fool André got himself caught. Our plan is foiled.

Peggy
André caught! What will happen to him?

Arnold
Think no more of him. He will hang, as will we both, unless we make speedy exit. Goodbye, my dear.
(*kisses her forehead goodbye and begins to leave*)

Peggy
Benny! Don't leave me!

Arnold
I must. In this time we must each look to ourselves and make our own escapes, I with my talents, you with yours. Adieu.
(*turning*)
Gentlemen, I must to the fortress to prepare it for the General's afternoon inspection. I'm sure, however, that Mrs. Arnold will be able to entertain you.

(*Exit. Offstage is heard "Yaah!" and the sound of galloping hooves.*)

Officer
He certainly is ardent to please the General.

Peggy
(*nervously flirtatious*)
Ah yes, we Arnolds are all very...ardent.

(*Enter Washington*)

Peggy
(*beaming*)
General Washington!

Washington
(*kissing her hand*)
Mrs. Arnold, you are more beautiful than ever. I see you have all my young officers in love with you already. Where is your husband, General Arnold? I trust he is well?

Peggy
Oh yes, but you know Benedict, always on the move. As soon as he heard you were nigh he ran down to the fort to prepare it for your inspection.

Washington
Just like old Arnold!

(*Galloping hooves are heard, followed by the sound of a fast dismount. Enter Talmadge disheveled*)

Talmadge
General Washington!

Washington
Major Talmadge, this is somewhat irregular.

Talmadge
General, I must speak to you alone this instant.

Washington
I trust this is important...Very well.

(*They go aside. Talmadge explains animatedly, shows the letter and the plans. A look of horror grows on Washington's face.*)

Washington
(*to everyone*)
Arnold has betrayed us!

(*Peggy faints theatrically and is caught by Hamilton and Varick. Washington ignores her.*)

Washington
Colonel Hamilton! Take horse at once! Catch him! He mustn't escape!

Hamilton
Yes sir
(*disentangling himself from Peggy*).

(*exit; galloping hooves*)

Washington
(*addressing other officer*)
You sir, pass the word to alert the fort, then ride with all haste to General Greene commanding our army at Tappan. Tell him to make forced march to reach West Point this very night. If Arnold sent a second messenger we can expect a British attack up the river before dawn.

Officer
Yes sir!
(*rapid exit*)

Washington
A dark day. Who can we trust now?
(*pause; notices Peggy*)
What's happened here?

Lafayette
The poor creature is stricken with grief.

Peggy
(*awakening, putting her hands softly on Varick's cheeks*)
Colonel Varick, don't kill my child, my poor little innocent child.

Varick
Don't be afraid, Madam, no harm is going to come to your child.

Peggy
Oh, my poor little baby, only General Washington can save my poor little baby!

Varick
This is General Washington.

Peggy
No he's not. He is the man who is going to help Colonel Varick kill my child.

Lafayette
The poor angel is mad with grief, yet can think of nothing but saving her child!

Washington
(*taking her up gently*)
Don't worry child. I am General Washington and no one is going to hurt you or your baby.

Peggy
(*fondling his hair locks, cheeks, etc., sobbing seductively into his face, etc.*)
Then you'll be kind to my poor little baby, my poor, poor little baby.

Washington
(*holding her protectively*)
There, there, that's better; you're safe now, your baby is safe, everything's going to be alright.

Varick
I'll help her to her room.
(*gently escorts her out*)

Lafayette
To think that such beautiful innocence should have married a traitor! Such angelic loveliness together with such evil. Who would believe it?

(*Washington nods gravely and all exeunt*)

John André after his capture. Self portrait.

Act V Scene V

(*Scene: Washington's headquarters near Tappan*)
(*Enter Hamilton and Elizabeth Schuyler*)

Elizabeth
And you believe her innocent?

Hamilton
Entirely. No one who witnessed her agony could doubt it. One moment she raved, another she melted into tears. Sometimes she pressed her infant to her bosom and lamented its fate occasioned by the imprudence of its father, in a manner that would have pierced insensibility itself. All the sweetness of beauty, all the loveliness of innocence, all the tenderness of a wife, and all the fondness of a mother show themselves in her appearance and conduct.

Elizabeth
She is ill?

Hamilton
Yes.

Elizabeth
So she receives you only by her bedside.

Hamilton
Yes.

Elizabeth
(*aside*)
A good choice.
(*to Hamilton*)
But though she be sick, she keeps herself neatly groomed?

Hamilton
Her face and hair, well enough, but she is so frantic with distress that she does not realize she is but scantily clothed during the interview, and so mad she is that her servant cannot make her clothe or cover herself.

Elizabeth
(*aside*)
And with sweet visions doth make you blind.
Poor Alexander, your wit is no match for her charms, but that is fine;
Once we're wed, you'll be no match for mine.

Hamilton
And this Major André is such a gallant officer.

Elizabeth
Indeed he is, gracious, and refined. Is there any way he can be saved?

Hamilton
So I dearly hope. Thus, with the General's permission, I have writ to Clinton asking exchange of Arnold for André.

(*enter Washington during this remark*)

Washington
Which he has refused. As could have been foreseen. Were Clinton to give Arnold to our gallows, never again would a traitor cross the lines, and in treason alone do British hopes now lie.

Hamilton
So André must hang?

Washington
Yes. And now I wish to meet alone with the prisoner. Have him brought hence, Colonel.

(*exit Hamilton*)

Begging your pardon, Miss Schuyler.

Elizabeth
Oh, I quite understand, General.
(*exit*)

(*reenter Hamilton with André*)

Washington
If you would be good enough to wait outside, Colonel.

Hamilton
Yes Sir.
(*exit*)

Washington
So, Major André, it is my duty to inform you that it is the unanimous sentence of the trial board that you are a spy and that you be sentenced to hang as such. I have approved the sentence.

André
You would hang a gentleman of my quality as a spy?

Washington
Nathan Hale was hung as a spy.

André
Hale? Hale was a school teacher! The cases are in no way comparable.

Washington
I fail to see how the differences are to your credit.

André
Why should I hang for Arnold's crime?

Washington
I would gladly exchange you for he, as would greatly be to our advantage. But Clinton is not so foolish. However it must be said that in the eye of Justice you are seen as far more guilty than Arnold, for you were the source of his crime.

André
What I did was in honorable service to my King.

Washington
Your service was not honorable, nor is your King.

André
You realize the favor the crown would hold you in should you secure my release.

Washington
You insult me, sir.

André
(*aside*)
This man is a fanatic and must be used as such. Wrath may capture such men, as lusts mislead others. I may hang, but before I do, I'll trick him into an angry act that will wreck his cause.
(*to Washington*)
So then, hang me if it suits your spite, but let Peggy Arnold go. She's innocent, you may count on that. I give you my word, innocent as a lamb, even if she is sympathetic to the King's cause.

Washington
Have no fear for her. She is free to go.

André
(*aside*)
The fool suspects nothing even when I drop such clues. I'll be more obvious.
(*to Washington*)
If anyone suspects her innocence let them read the many letters she and I exchanged. Nay, I insist that you read them, so you may be assured of her innocence.

Washington
There's no need of that.

André
(*aside*)
What a dunce! I better tell him outright.
(*to Washington*)
Hah hah, you are a fool.

Washington
How so?

André
You think her innocent, yet it was through her that I broke Arnold's will and made him a traitor. She is as guilty as sin itself.

Washington
I know that.

André
You know! You know that it was she and she alone through whom I was able to wreck your first of men, and yet you would let her go?

Washington
A beautiful martyr is a dangerous enemy. I see no need to supply the King with such an ally.

André
(*aside*)
Damn!
(*to Washington*) :
(*pause*)
I hate you!

Washington
I know that.

André
(*pause*)
Just what do you hope to accomplish anyhow?

Washington
You mean if victorious in this war?

André
Yes.

Washington
I hope to found an empire of reason, where men will be free to frame their own laws and so secure the justest and happiest government.

André
What you propose is anarchy. Men cannot rule themselves.

Washington
Good men can, men who believe in justice and truth and who will stand by what they know to be right.

André
Such men exist only in the upper class, and even there are but a handful. The mass of men are ruled by greed, not principle, and so will and must be ruled by those with wealth to pay their little treats.

Washington
Your captors were poor men, yet could not be bought.

André
Three fanatical ruffians, anxious for revenge. What do they signify?

Washington
My army fights for principle, not gain.

André
They are men passioned by the heat of the present struggle. With such men you may win this round, but it will not last
With peace such heroic feelings will fade and corruption seep in every crack. Thus will your proud republic fall to an early ruin. For the virtue of the fathers will not last in the sons. And we shall return, to rule. Whether from without or within, it will make no difference.

Washington
We shall see, Major André. Colonel Hamilton!

(*Enter Hamilton*)

Hamilton
Yes sir!

Washington
Take this man back to his cell and prepare him to be hung at dawn.

André
You may hang me, General Washington, but the world belongs to me and men like me. It always has and it always will. It may take years, it may take centuries, but in the end your cause is doomed.

Washington
Take him away.

Hamilton
Yes sir!

(*escorts André out.*)

Washington
For such men God made hell
We have beat them, but only time will tell
Will our virtue fade and republic crumble?
He may be right.
On that future ages must shed their light.
And so, fellow citizens, good night!

(*exit*)

THE END

General George Washington, Painting by Charles Wilson Peale.

Notes on the Play

This play is a drama of history. All the principle characters were real people, and all the principle events and interactions between the characters are entirely true to fact.

At the time of the start of the play (1777), the ages of the characters were as follows: George Washington, 45; Benedict Arnold, 36, Major John André, 27, Alexander Hamilton, 22, Marquis de Lafayette, 20, Peggy Shippen, 17.

Major General Benedict Arnold was arguably the best combat officer on either side during the American Revolution. His achievements included capturing Fort Ticonderoga near the start of the war, an action which provided George Washington with the cannon needed to take Boston from the British. He then led an army in an epic march across the Maine wilderness in late autumn, almost capturing the British stronghold of Quebec by surprise, and then besieging it throughout the winter with an inferior force. Retreating into New York in 1776, he built a fleet of ships on Lake Champlain, manned them with militia, and stopped a British invasion flotilla by fighting them to a mutually devastating draw in the battle of Valcour Island. After fighting other notable actions, Arnold traveled south, and met with George Washington encamped along the Delaware with the remains of his army during December 1776. There is good reason to believe that it was Arnold who suggested the daring counterstroke of gambling the remnants of the Continental Army in a surprise midnight attack across the Delaware on Christmas Eve, 1776— an action which saved the American cause in its darkest hour. Most famously, it was Arnold, who, without command authority, rallied fleeing American forces on the field at Saratoga to deliver a counterattack that smashed Burgoyne, decisively changing the course of the war.

Arnold, however, was of humble social origins. His family had no status and he had worked in such unprestigious occupations as drugstore clerk before the war. His primary ambition was to make his way into the colonial upper crust. This made him susceptible to targeting for corruption and reversal by British intelligence.

Major John André was the head of British intelligence for North America. Because of his dramatic death upon the scaffold, his charming social accomplishments, and his close connections with poetess Anna Seward and other major literary figures in England who painted a glowing picture of him afterwards, André has come down to us in romantic histories as a tragic hero, a good and brave young man "who died for Arnold's crime." In fact, nothing could be further from the truth. A member of a wealthy Swiss banking family and owner of large landholdings on the island of Grenada, André was a fanatical enemy of the American Revolution, which he considered a threat to the world's social order. In discussions among British officers he advocated murder of all American combatants taken prisoner, and at massacres at Tappan and Paoli he led British forces which did exactly that. Because of this, André was viewed with distain by many regular British Army officers, who also did not like him because of the way he had used both his money and a sycophantic relationship with (North American theater commander) General Sir Henry Clinton to climb his way to the top of the military social structure.

André's methods of obtaining intelligence combined mobilizing networks of Tory sympathizers with directing bribes to leading personalities in the Patriot camp. While in Philadelphia during the British winter 1777-78 occupation of that city, André met and established a relationship with Peggy Shippen. Before he left town the following spring (with the book collection he stole from Ben Franklin's personal library), André had recruited Peggy as a spy for British intelligence.

Peggy Shippen was one of the top Tory belles in Pennsylvania.

The Shippen family owned a significant fraction of the colony, and despite her age (17 in 1777) and sex, the forceful Peggy was already playing a major role in running the family's financial affairs at the time she met André. While at the peak of the colonial social pyramid, Peggy longed to be part of real aristocracy, thus her fascination with André. She also was a thoroughly committed Tory. While some radical elements on the revolutionary political scene did accuse her at the time of being complicit with Arnold when his treason was discovered, romantic historians have generally portrayed her as the beautiful innocent angel who was betrayed by the beast.

In fact, the radicals were right. We know this from two sources. In the first place, on her way back from West Point to Philadelphia after the plot failed, Peggy stopped at the house of her cousin, Theodosia Prevost (the future wife of the scoundrel Aaron Burr.) As soon as the accompanying males were out of their presence, Peggy dropped her pretense of being insane with sorrow, and, bragging that she had run the whole affair, told everything to Theodosia (who was also a Tory). In 1830, on the 50th anniversary of the Arnold affair, Burr's biographer published a magazine article in which he revealed this. That would still leave room for doubt. However in 1933, 150 years after the Treaty of Paris ended hostilities, the British government felt it was finally safe to declassify their archives on secret operations in North America during the war. Columbia University historian Carl Van Doren traveled to England to review the archives, and there he found the letters Peggy had sent to André in invisible ink. He published these findings in his book "The Secret History of the American Revolution" in 1941.

After the war, Peggy and Arnold relocated to England, where he was despised and she was pitied for having thrown herself away on such a low-born person. Arnold became a merchant ship captain, and in 1793 was captured in the Caribbean by a French frigate. He escaped by breaking through the hull of a prison ship and swimming two miles across shark-infested waters to reach a British held island.

Arnold died, nearly bankrupt, in 1801. According to Peggy, "The disappointment of all his pecuniary expectations...so broke his spirit that he literally fell sacrifice to a perturbed mind." Using her charm and social connections, Peggy was able to induce Lord Cornwallis to save the family from bankruptcy, but she fell victim to uterine cancer and died in 1804 at the age of 44.

Major Benjamin Talmadge had a successful political career, and in 1830 was U.S. Senator from Connecticut. Because of the 50th anniversary, there was a motion made in Congress to grant veteran's pensions to the three skinners who had caught André; Paulding, Van Wart, and Williams, who were all still alive. Talmadge protested vigorously that he had known these people, and that they were just bandits out looting while real soldiers were making much greater sacrifices. No one listened to him, and the skinners got their pensions.

In 1830, the British acted on their view of André as martyr, and had his remains relocated to Westminster Abbey. In 1880, on the 100th anniversary of the Arnold affair, they attempted to carry this tradition a step further by erecting a statue of André under the tree near West Point where he was hung, just like the statue of Nathan Hale in lower Manhattan. The statue was dynamited. Not to be intimidated, an anglophile committee had the statue rebuilt and put back in place. It was dynamited again. So they made a plaque and put it there instead. It is still there today.

Notes on the Songs

"The Banks of the Dee," was the most popular song among Tories during the American Revolution, inspiring numerous parodies on the Patriot side. It is not known if Peggy sang for André, but if she had, "The Banks of the Dee" would almost certainly have been among those performed.

"How Stands the Glass Around" was a drinking song popular among British officers. Expressing a devil-may-care attitude towards death, (we're all going to die, who cares, pass the drinks, etc.) it actually was sung by General Wolfe at a party of British officers on the night before the Battle of Quebec. The British triumph the next day won Canada for the Crown, but Wolfe was killed. On the night before he went up the river to meet Arnold, André imitated Wolfe, and, striking a heroic pose, climbed up on the table of a New York tavern to sing the song to a party of British officers, exactly as depicted in the play.

Originating in the Anacreonic Club in London, by 1780 "To Anacreon in Heaven" was a popular party song in both Britain and America, among Patriots and Tories alike. It remained popular for decades, but achieved true immortality in 1814, when Francis Scott Key reworded it with new lyrics to become "The Star Spangled Banner."

About the Author

Dr. Robert Zubrin is an internationally renowned astronautical engineer and the acclaimed author of *The Case for Mars*, which Arthur C. Clarke called "the most comprehensive account of the past and future of Mars that I have ever encountered." NASA has adopted many of the features of Zubrin's humans-to-Mars mission plan. A former senior engineer at Lockheed Martin, Zubrin is president of the Mars Society, a non-profit group promoting planetary exploration, and founder of Pioneer Astronautics, a successful space technology research and development firm. Zubrin is the author of over 150 technical and non-technical papers in the areas of space exploration and nuclear engineering, and holds two US patents. His other books include the non-fiction *Entering Space: Creating a Spacefaring Civilization*, and *Mars on Earth*, the hard science fiction novel *First Landing*, and *The Holy Land,* a science fiction satire on contemporary events. *Benedict Arnold* is his first historical drama.

Commenting on *Benedict Arnold*, Zubrin said, "The American Revolution has always fascinated me, because it was a moment that a people rose above its apparent practical self-interest to launch and win a fight for a visionary future. The key struggle was more moral than military. Arnold sold out, but, miraculously, most of his fellow Continentals did not. That miracle carries message of real hope and challenge for our kind. It dares us to be great."

Dr. Zubrin lives with his family in Colorado.